Bonards Caprice

Writing by: BINGKAI SHAN

Gun Rights as a Trinity In U.S.A

We live in the world is sinful, Tragedy is the norm! People only admit mistakes

The United States of American citizens have the right to own guns, which is a very important right of There. People have support it, and who make oppose it. Every time someone shoots innocent people with guns, a call to ban citizens from holding guns grows. People naively think

that if everyone doesn't have the right to privately own a gun, then, of course, this madman-like behavior swept through a crowd with a gun, there will no longer be a chance.

However, this view does not convince all people, a murderer who wants to kill, if there is no gun, can choose a knife, or choose a car, in fact, he may have other options, such a person drives a big truck into the Crowds, this kind of lethality may not be less than the lethality of a gun, do we need to discuss the right to ban everyone from owning a car one day?

The related debate here constitutes diversity, and no one can convince the other, so Americans have been arguing about citizens' rights to bear guns for many years, which constitutes a big issue in the management of American society. Moreover, Americans still insist that, compared with other factors, one's right to own a gun is still one of the most important rights.

Why is this happening? Why do Americans still insist that citizens have the right to legally own guns when almost all countries in the world have banned guns. In fact, this involves people's comprehensive understanding of gun rights. Because it is based on the traditional American Christian culture and American institutional design, the power of citizens is actually a public phenomenon of the Trinity Model.

The first order is that individual rights take precedence. That is, any citizen of the United States has the right to protect his personal rights through the right to own a gun.

The second order, the primary purpose of individual gun rights, is to protect individuals in vulnerable situations against powerful government violence with their guns in their hands. In other words, the primary purpose of American gun rights is to monitor possible coercive behavior by the government.

Third order, fair use of personal gun rights. This is the essence of an order with a very traditional American spirit, that is, the traditional American society believes that a person can become a "prudent" person in an ethical sense based on his belief in God. A U.S. citizen in the traditional sense can use his gun rights reasonably, legally, and prudently.

The above three orders constitute the comprehensive essence of American gun rights, which is expressed as a "three-one model". Through the current analysis, we believe that the first order, the priority of individual rights, is not controversial, and any civilized country should respect individual rights as the first principle. The second order, the principle of individual supervision and restraint of the government, is also the norm in civilized countries, so there is no dispute.

The problem lies in the Third Order, which contains a basic problem: after a natural person legally holds a gun, how can he ensure that he can use the gun reasonably and prudently, and how can he control his inner motive for murder. To answer this basic question, also face a trinity order:

First order, a person can reasonably use the right to bear a gun based on his principle of adherence to the law;

In the second order, a person can reasonably use the right to bear a gun based on the principle of calculating his own interests;

Third order, a person can reasonably use the right to bear a gun based on the principle of his own fear of God;

That is to say, only when a person integrates the three elements of law, self-interest, and fear of God into his own conceptual order, he can control his impulses and use his gun rights rationally.

In the same way, in this Trinity order, the first order and the second order are both human rational abilities. When a person is rationally aware of the punishment mechanism of the law and his own interests, he may be able to rationally use the gun rights. But common sense tells us that people's rational ability is limited, there is a minimal boundary order, and rational ability may lead to conceit. When one crosses the boundaries of reason, when one's reason moves toward fatal conceit, the seriousness of the law and the calculation of interests no longer have the *necessary prudent effect on one's actions, and such a person will do unbearable evil.*

Therefore, under the traditional cultural background of the United States building a country with Christianity, a person must have comprehensive individual autonomy in terms of the three elements of law, interests, and Christian belief, and must return to the conservative cultural order based on Christian belief. among.

If Christianity has been regarded by Americans as a backward and unfree way of thinking and way of life, if conservatism has become a value phenomenon that is ridiculed by people in the United States, if those who hold to Christianity and the spirit of conservatism are no longer If you stick to your beliefs and be ashamed of the gospel, then your right to own guns will become your right to commit evil and kill people recklessly.

Such an analysis brings us a methodology for judging American society so that we finally understand why politicians like Obama and Hillary always try to disqualify American citizens from legal gun rights because they have left conservative Christianity, Stop believing that God constitutes an order of censorship over each individual's mind. When a politician stops believing the adage, "The Lord alone watches the heart," it manifests itself in their absolute distrust of all citizens, instead of believing that only the coercive power of government constitutes evil control over everyone.

Here, people's hidden institutional concept is the belief that the government is perfect, moderate, and a public institution worthy of everyone's trust. That is to say, they believe that a government that serves the well-being of all people does not have the evil order of human nature. This kind of perception phenomenon is the norm in almost all authoritarian countries, so our analysis implies a major trend. When Democrats are racking their brains to deprive American citizens of the right to bear guns, in fact, the United States is not far from authoritarian countries.

But the Democrats' conceptual order, of course, is not acceptable to those with conservative traditions. From this, we finally understand some phenomena in American society, such as why Republicans like President Reagan, even though he was shot by a killer and almost died, still insisted on defending the right of American citizens to bear guns, because Reagan believed that when the Christian faith is the way of the people The order is solid enough that when the spirit of conservatism becomes the consensus of the majority of the American people, politicians believe that American citizens have the individual autonomy of the reasonable use of gun rights. And for the very few perpetrators who abuse guns and kill innocents, politicians believe that the power of law can be limited in their solution.

These are the values of a true conservative Republican, A wise politician, when dealing with the proposition of private gun rights, must adhere to the Trinity Order, which not only protects the rights of individuals but also monitors the violence of the government. A return to traditional Christian spirit and conservative values. When we do this, we will get a least bad country, not an absolutely perfect country.

Objectives &Processes

On the Comprehensive Judgment

Bravery is one of the ethical attributes of human beings, but the ethical concept of bravery itself is neutral. If a person is unstable in the sense of the ultimate concept, then one's bravery is likely to be a reckless, destructive sacrifice of evil.

Thinkers have debated the ethical concept of bravery for thousands of years. Aristotle first put forward the ethical content of bravery in "Nicomacus Ethics": "Brave is the power of an act in the face of fear." Later, Aquinas defined the ethical definition of bravery. Explaining that he translated Aristotle's writings into Latin, and believed that the thousands-long Christian tradition of "martyrdom" is the most stable and ultimate definition of "brave": brave because of the truth.

As a result, when people discuss the ethical spirit of "braveness", they will cite the facts of martyrs in Christian history. People try to prove that truth is the cause of one's bravery and the purpose of one's bravery. Only those Christians who believe in the truth have the strength to truly refrain from cooperating with power, although not all Christians do.

In this absurd country and in absurd times, there are indeed some Christians who have kept their faith to the death. In this day and age, talented people are disobeying the Christian faith, brave people who would rather go to jail than make any compromises.

Among all the shortcomings of human beings, a hypocrite is the most harmful, causing people to live in hell forever, with almost no possibility of renewal. Jesus' criticism and curse of the hypocrisy of the Pharisees were decisive and cruel. Chinese cultural tradition is originally a "hypocritical" tradition. In the past, we demonstrated our hypocrisy under the traditional concept of "benevolence, righteousness, courtesy, wisdom, and trustworthiness". This constitutes our "original position" and constitutes the origin of a concept and behavior. origin.

If he is fortunate enough to be chosen by God to become a Christian, it is very likely that one of the first signs of humanity he learns is Jewish *hypocrisy. The hypocrisy of humanity and the hypocrisy of the Pharisees have a huge resonance in our religious life. If we don't quickly realize that the sacrifice that God wants is a broken heart and a broken spirit, then our Christian religious life will be driven by hypocrisy.*

Due to the limitation of time and space, people always try their best to create a visible goal for themselves, so as to comfort their short understanding ability. Confucius took Zhou as the goal, Confucianism took Confucius as the goal, Islamic believers aimed at heaven on earth, Buddhist believers aimed at becoming Buddhas themselves, Kant aimed at people, and Christians aimed at visible miracles. Look closely at people's purpose orientation, and you'll admit that everyone is short-sighted.

Yes everyone should think about what they are aiming for. Dante said, in the middle of my life, I lost the truth and fell asleep. This is a kind of self-recognition, a kind of repentance, a lamentation dedicated to oneself, and a fact of human nature. Our so-called life has always been looking for excuses for our laziness and shortsightedness. If God is not our goal, then we must die halfway.

Kierkegaard said that people who truly aim at God in human society are extremely rare, and most people are stuck in a vulgar place in the middle. This is his extreme suspicion of the finiteness of human nature. So he left his last words, and the pastor of his church is not allowed to preside over his funeral after his death, because in his opinion, it is impossible to find people like Abraham who really aim at God in life. The familiar priests of, but in the name of priests, consumption in this world. Surprisingly, the priest Kierkegaard was referring to turned out to be his own brother.

Descartes believed that the methodology of human beings is to doubt, and many people think that the doubts launched by Descartes are to doubt God, but Augustine stated very early that the only people who should always be doubted are people. Descartes, of course, was well aware of this truth, so he always doubted people.

Radical skepticism of man is a stable tradition of the Christian faith. A careful reading of the Gospels reveals that Jesus had a complete distrust of human nature, no matter how much people shouted the name of God, how firmly they expressed their stronger faith. Jesus would say, you always do not believe.

Unbelief, little faith, and irrepressible little faith are the normal state of human nature. Those who have never known God are unbelievers. Those who are chosen Christians are little faith. Human nature is incurable in a general sense.

Doubt about human nature must be pushed to the point of incurable, otherwise, all beliefs are to satisfy one's own narrow mind. I'm going to put *it a bit harsher. People who always emphasize their confidence are usually covering up their darkness. The sad thing about us is that when we became Christians, we did learn to praise God, but we never learned to doubt ourselves.*

All wisdom and knowledge come from doubting people. A person who does not doubt himself is ignorant. When this ignorance develops to the level of hypocrisy, in fact, the hymn he dedicates to God may also be hypocritical.

Faith is really important, and without full faith, we cannot be saved by Jesus, and in this sense justification by faith is a perfectly correct statement. But this is a statement in a result-oriented sense, not a process sense. In a result-

oriented sense, when we die, when our bodies disappear, Jesus' redemption must become a fact because of our faith. This is all we are born to hope for. But in the sense of process, in the sense of pilgrimage and sojourn, we must doubt ourselves as much as Jesus doubted us, expand our horizons, and unfold the great open-ended error correction.

When emphasizing the process, emphasize the ultimate goal. When we emphasize the ultimate goal, we want to emphasize the process.

The Great faith can allow us to store in the depths of our hearts a synthesis of the ultimate goal and the meaning of the process.

Simple Belief Is Only Prerequisite

A person to enter the biblical order

Man is a man of free will created by God, and there is doubt where there is doubt, and it is the basic mental attitude of man. To believe or to doubt, that is the question.

The emergence of knowledge into simple belief is a given of wisdom and a blessing of knowledge. People who have the ability to put forward hypothetical premises first, such as Newton put forward the first driving force. From simple belief to the hypothetical premise, this is the greatest mystery, the driving force of the human mind.

The Confucian assumption of human nature is benevolence, the methodology is filial piety, the goal is the Tao of Heaven, and the concept of personality is the gentleman and the villain. This is a set of moral philosophies. The problem is not the downward institutional design of Confucianism, but the initialization of the Dao of Heaven, the unidirectionalization of human nature, the externalization of personality, and the use of filial piety to cover all areas. The Confucian tradition does not simply believe in the Tao of Heaven but in the self-statement of human beings. Therefore, in the context of culture, filial piety is not only a family concept, a cultural concept but also a political concept and a national concept. Filial piety is no longer an emotional resonance, but the control and slavery between people.

Criticizing human nature must believe in advance that there are clear benchmark conditions and frames of reference higher than human nature, otherwise all discussions about human nature will be neither scientific nor profound. Our eyes were covered with a huge black cotton cloth.

Then, I could speak, and I would burst into tears, or be heartbroken. It's a miracle. It's incredible, not a tree downstairs, nor a stray dog in the street. This is the greatest grace God has given me, and it is also the limit of freedom that God has set for me.

If people can't speak, they also lose their freedom. To deprive a man of his right to speak is to deprive him of all his powers.

God is both the creator of truth and the speaker of truth. Truth and discourse form two sides of one body. Truth and God on the one hand, and the Word of God on the other. The truth is hidden, the word is present. The world is primarily driven by discourse. Logos, Word, Tao, these words in different contexts that contain the dual meanings of truth and speech at the same time.

Postmodern philosophy is actually a struggle against God's created order. Whether it is Derrida's "difference" or Husserl's "epoch", it is a struggle against the Logos tradition. This is the ideological historical landscape that must appear after rationalism matures. Going back to the biblical tradition for observation, it is probably similar to Jacob wrestling with an angel in the wilderness. On the surface, it seems that man and angel can be tied, but unfortunately, man has a prior human defect, which leads to human beings must dance with tragedy. In this way, today's seemingly high-tech and seemingly knowledge-exploding era may be a truly tragic era. If you don't bring yourself to the brink of destruction, you won't let it go.

No matter what issues you think about, you can't forget that people are the most important thing in the world so God will die on the cross for the eternal hope of human life. There are many people in life who never realize the absolute importance of human beings innately, when they think about it, they are most prone to make the mistake of putting the meaning of human beings, human values, human rights, and human rights for various reasons. Life looks down. This is ideological propaganda that we are familiar with, such as sacrificing a person's life for the sake of the country, taking away a person's freedom for money, shooting unarmed people for social stability, and so on.

This is the most obvious guilt, but the beginning of sin comes from the instability of values, from our neglect of the most basic common sense in this world made up of people. The sad thing is that the seemingly ignorant society wastes life, and no matter how developed the society is, it wastes life. Human society has so far not understood the absolute command of God, and as human beings, we have not yet developed a basic knowledge about human beings.

Whistleblower of Times

Greatest Evil Lies in Confidence and Unrepentance.

Judas is the culmination of human whistleblower behavior. In the dimension of intellectual history, Judas is the coordinate of the whistleblower and a totem of whistleblower behavior. This means that various states of whistle-blowing will always appear in human minds and behaviors, and whistle-blowing has become a rational choice for human behavior and a model tool for people to do evil.

At the beginning of AD time, Judas seemed to still be ashamed, so two bright spots remained in his behavior. The first was to return the bribes of the Pharisees and the blood money; the second was to commit suicide and hang himself to death.

Looking back at the whistleblowers of our time, would they return their blood money, would they be so ashamed that they hanged themselves?

The depravity of the human mind and behavior is an iron fact. Judas of today's age is far less gentle than the Judas of the past. The human condition *is not getting better, but getting worse. If people in the past did evil, there may still be some bottom lines, then today's evil is not the worst, only the worst.*

It is a pity that today's young people are so handy in playing informative skills, and even the little bit of shame left by Judas has been completely lost.

But we need Judas in our time, and if there is no Judas, who will send us to prison? So we want to thank the informers in this era. It is their behavior that makes us begin to realize our powerlessness, start to leave the false role of enlightened people, start to learn to carry the cross on our body, start to truly appreciate the wound of the whip, and start to embrace

punishment deep peace.

Only when a person truly appreciates the
importance of the cross as the coordinate system
of life will he begin to learn to think about himself
and this chaotic world. Yes, blessed are those who
always read the Bible and meditate on the Word
of God day and night because they are slowly
developing an intuitive judgment about the world,
about the human condition. It is this intuitive
judgment, rather than knowledge-based
judgment, that ensures that one does not end up
in ruin in the most absurd of times.

So dear friends, judgment from knowledge is
usually neutral, with a certain kind of short-

sighted utilitarianism attached to it. This is where we should wake up in our pursuit of knowledge.

Why has there always been a discussion about truth, this question leads people to either believe in the absolute existence of the ultimate truth, or aphasia and enter a long-term silent state of mind; when we understand this, relying on intuitive judgment, we find that Chinese intellectuals Perhaps the biggest mistake is not choosing to be silent after forgetting the truth, but falling into a long period of low-level expression.

The profound analysis of the dark state of human nature realizes that the biggest problem at present is that we have a seriously superficial understanding of ourselves, and the cultural system should not be of the times, mainly because we do not know ourselves. This question is timeless!

Finding solutions, believing that truth exists, is an open-ended error-correcting methodology unfolding against the murky nature of human nature. Critics will have the power to reach the level of individual people's minds. A true understanding of the order of public sentiments is the biggest factor in determining the direction of a country, and the true meaning of public sentiments order is in everyone's mind, not in the books of intellectuals.

Intellectuals are completely unable to enter the process of the problem and the problem of the process, denying the existence of the only truth. Once again confirmed the words of the Bible, the fear of Jehovah is the beginning of wisdom. Fantasy education enlightens the masses. How corrupt, or ignorant, is this ridiculous state?

When whistleblowers are concentrated in university classrooms, the darkness and shamelessness of an era is a kind of irony to intellectuals. I hope that a few of them can go through such a real ordeal and become aware of their powerlessness and ignorance, and then have the ability to go into their minds and start thinking about some important basic questions.

The Outbreak of the Warlords

The idea of communism was conceived by Marx. Revolutionaries, proletarians, and intellectuals are the greatest stupidity of the age.

The Outburst of Stupidity is the idea of justice theory conceived by Rawls. University professors, the media, and a large number of young people who are influenced by them are the three biggest fools of this era.

Stupid people, held hostage by evil, always bring great misery to the world.

The presence of intellectuals in both stupidities means that human misery is usually designed by intellectuals and then built by a group of rogue thugs. They constructed a beautiful goal, but the road to that goal was paved with corpses.

The fate of mankind as a whole rises and falls between these two stupidities.

After the European and American society defeated the Marxist communist thought with great difficulty, after a short recuperation, they fell into the self-justice theory of thought conceived by John Rawls relying on the superimposed consensus of human beings. In a trend sense, John Rawls's theory of self-justice would be more destructive than Marx's communist manifesto. John Rawls did not hide the importance he attached to Marx in ideological *inheritance. He even stated generously that Marx's thought was his most important source. What is terrifying is that in today's European and American society, those intellectuals who have thoroughly analyzed Marx have fallen headlong at the feet of John Rawls. With his thoughts as a foothold, he has constructed political correctness that looks beautiful.*

Only force capable of defeating two evil currents at the same time is traditional conservative Christianity. This is an era when ideas defeat ideas. Those Christian warriors with a bible in one hand and a sword in the other, the descendants of Joshua, those friends of Reagan, Thatcher, and Trump are the ones who will lead the world out of misery. large army.

Where are people with common sense and basic intuitive judgment in this era, among those who began to reflect on themselves after being enslaved? Therefore, among the traditional Christian folk order crowd in the United States, among the conservative crowd in the UK who are quietly advancing, and among the house church crowd in Eastern Europe, in Korea, and even in China who have been suppressed by the dictatorial government, we can always be able to see the figure of the Christian warrior. They were strong and courageous, and they were no longer afraid. They have faith, horses, and the stone in David's hand, and they will gain strength from the word of God to defeat the giants of this age.

Ethics in Life

Hedonism is an experience that is keen on the experience of life, and it is possible to express this experience in art. Such a life, in the subjective sense of human nature, has a certain ability of construction, including the ability to construct ideas, the ability to construct life, and the ability to construct art.

However, these construction capabilities are all at the moment and lack eternal vision, which is manifested in that people have no long-term responsibility, passion, and mission for the world. It is even believed that the world is full of possibilities, so people will consume life and consume the world as much as possible through thought, through life, and art, and thus obtain a certain level of aesthetic meaning in life. The so-called beauty of the Chinese people is actually in this dimension. Kierkegaard believes that in the world of human order, aesthetic life is a relatively low life state, and it is the spiritual appeal of a person in the first stage after he emerges from the animal world.

Efforts to get out of the aesthetic life and face sub-optimal solutions to real-world problems. To live more beautifully, one must take the necessary responsibility for the land, and one must understand the moral order and the ethical principles of human nature. The rational boundary order understands the limitations of human nature and recognizes human ignorance and powerlessness. In the face of things within the scope, full of irresistible questions and criticism. Ethical efforts and their sadness will make people suddenly lose the meaning of life, suddenly overestimate the meaning of life, and fall into a state of despair and conceit.

The life of faith leads to the eternal kingdom, but people can never reach it by the ability of reason.

Believers must complete Leap of Faith, leap from the dimension of ethics to the dimension of faith, use the power of faith to overcome the lingering sense of despair, confusion, and powerlessness of human nature, and overcome those that are generally considered impossible in human ethics. Things.

The existence of every person, the existence of every kind of thought, must be in one dimension.

Some people devote their whole lives to the aesthetic life, some people devote their whole lives to the ethical life, and some people devote their whole lives to the faith life. Everyone's life is partial, and Kierkegaard gave three propositions:

Only a clear belief in God can give limited people hope that "everything is possible";

Abraham is a model of the life of faith, he is the "father of faith";

Abraham's life is the fragmentation and transcendence of human ethics.

This is a stable Trinity model of ethics. In Fear and Trembling, Kierkegaard gave enough presentation and analysis of Abraham's life. Abraham, our "father of faith", obeyed God's call to kill his son and offer burnt offerings. Such dilemmas in life constitute a series of analyses and questions:

- If Abraham did not pay attention to the life and death of his son, then he was a common killer;

- If Abraham had no spiritual struggle in the moral sense, then he was a complete devil;

- If Abraham thought that he obeyed God's command to kill his son was merely an ethical principle, then he was a prop of God, and what he did would not constitute any meaning of life.

Abraham started from the meaning of ethics, finally transcended ethics, and fulfilled ethics is broken and transcended ways. Life leaps to a life of faith. Believe in the power of God, believe that all things are possible, believe in a vision, believe in eternity.

The linear ethics of meaning transcends aesthetics, and belief transcends ethics. The linear emergence process is based on this.

To live in this world is far from enough to have an aesthetic life. Roughness and inferiority must have an ethical meaning. If ethics collapse, the real world collapses. Towards hypocrisy, the transcendental meaning of faith.

Nowadays Anti-Social Tendency

I believe that history will remember the Covid-19 virus for a long time, not only to record the evil of China, but also to comprehensively record the shamelessness of human science, and record that people in this era have collectively turned into laboratory mice. The vaccines that are clearly marked as experimental products have not undergone thorough scientific experiments and demonstrations. Politicians in this era have begun to forcibly inject this experimental vaccine into people's bodies.

There is some absurdity and some collective stupidity. Darwin's theory of evolution has brought huge damage to the human value lineage. The reality of this thought is more and more understood by people. The thought that is more destructive than Darwin's thought is David Hume's animal rationality, which is about animal rationality. Construction, through the systematization and application of economics by economist Keynes, has almost brought human society into the darkest age in history.

Human rational conceit runs wildly along the path of animal rationality so that animal rationality has become the greatest political correctness of our time. Therefore, we can definitely believe that the so-called animal rational thought trend, which is very popular in the modern sense, is a hidden evil against humanity.

We think that a tree has a nervous system, but this belongs to the realm of physics, not thought and intelligence, and it has no soul. Science is possible because there is always an equilibrium and equilibrium of knowledge, such as the speed of light, the speed on Earth, and the speed in outer space, which is stable. This constitutes an equilibrium condition for scientific research.

We cannot use this scientific equilibrium thinking to deal with human nature, because human nature is the carrier of a soul, and human nature has been in a state of uncertainty and non-equilibrium for a long time. As the Bible reveals, the human heart is deceitful above all things, and human beings can never fully understand human nature except God. Therefore, human beings cannot use the scientific general equilibrium thinking to study human beings themselves.

This is most importantly common sense. Science is the study of physical objects, biblical discourse is the laying out of the human soul landscape, and the theory of human nature is the study of human thought and wisdom. People often conflate these important principles. If we assume that animals have a capacity for thinking similar to human nature, a capacity for human language intelligence, or even a capacity for the grief of the soul, then we must agree that the animal world can too. Develop a system of civilization that is homogenous to our own. Conversely, that is to say, when we find that it is impossible for animals to develop a human civilization system, it means that human intelligence and animal intelligence are not in a balanced condition, so the scientific ability of animals cannot be possible.

Although science claims to be prosperous and developed, so far it has not found the slightest existence similar to human civilization in the depths of the universe. Human civilization on earth hangs lonely like a lonely seed in the vast universe. Some people once thought that the shape of the earth's civilization is unique, and there must be civilizations on other planets, but the shape is completely different. When people on earth try to find civilizations on other planets, the civilization concepts they use are only those of the earth. Human scientists are not smart, they always compress deeper and greater things into the narrow human brain.

The funny thing is that human's understanding of animals is also forced to interpret animals as human beings. When philosophers invented the concept of rationality, they were finally anxious to understand animals as rational beings. This is the ideological predicament of the current society. When people want to expand their authority, they often understand living people with souls as animals; when they want to expand their knowledge, they often understand animals as living beings with souls. people. The shamelessness and corruption of human beings have finally developed to the extent of committing evil without a bottom line in the name of science.

The research approach of neurons in modern brain science is actually scientific research that first defines human beings as animal rationality. At first, they used animals as experimental objects to forcibly search for rationality in the animal world; The argument of beauty pulls people down to the dimension of the existence of animals, and thus conducts scientific research with human beings as experimental objects. Man is no longer a noble being specially created by God, but a guinea pig in a laboratory. As a result, scientists no longer take the human soul as a fact for granted and no longer believe in the breath of life breathed by God from the nose of human beings. They found a new scientific term, "neurons" that exist in animals and people.

It is precisely in the concept of "neuron" that a living person with a soul has a huge ideological divergence from modern brain science. Modern scientists are such a group of people that they lack the inheritance of beliefs, the profound understanding of the soul, and the cognition of the complexity of human life. They only understand human beings as scientific objects. In fact, neurons happen to be rational judgments of animals, while humans are living beings with souls, which constitutes a huge ambiguity in contemporary brain research.

The existence of ambiguity prevents us from discussing. A neuron is just a physical phenomenon and can be studied and subdivided. Brain science is thus possible. But once brain science becomes a fact, its research object will not be animal rationality, but the human brain and the human brain must be the research object. That is to say, the concept of animal rationality stated by the philosopher Hume has lost its basic meaning here. The reason why scientists continue to use the concept of animal rationality is just to find a plausible reason for them to use humans as a laboratory test.

Modern scholars have secretly carried out a shameless conceptual replacement here and invented a set of theories that are close to evil: animal rationality is equal to human rationality, and human brains are equal to animal brains.

The danger of human rational conceit is that when we interpret human brains as animal brains, we reduce the meaning of human beings and enter into the great evil against humanity in the name of science.

A Balanced Trinity Order

Discuss any proposition, we are three propositions, the greatest way of thinking, I'm going to listen, meditate , practice.

How to deal with the proposition of everything!

All things work together, First level of order is so important, the Bible has always stated that "all things work together", which means that we have to work hard, do things with all our heart, and everyone is born with the responsibility of the work, Passion, and mission.

Christians have a strong sense of charity, God gives everyone a talent, a kind of grace, and talent shine and increase income.

In Christian values, a loss is unacceptable and corruption is unacceptable, so everyone must have a broad enough imagination and capacity.

On the premise of valuing all things, the Bible advises us to "recognize all things as rubbish," which means that we should not be attached to the world. Our true and ultimate purpose is to come to Christ. People's nostalgia for everything in the world is an absolutely futile way of thinking and behavior. People will die without any accident.

When I stop breathing I cannot take any.

When presented separately culture emphasis could plunge one into ignorance. A third proposition arises, namely, how do we synthesize the two orders and constitute a paradox. Faced with such a paradox, a rational person cannot handle it properly.

Entrusting to God

Man's methodology here is consignment, not dialectics. Commitment to God is the great wisdom of man, while the dialectics imagined by philosophers is the rational conceit of human beings. Any dialectics on reason and behavior is a complete conceit of human nature.

By committing to God could people expand their realm and see a richer and more profound world.

The proposition of constitutes the third order in the Trinity order is truly hold the three orders together is the Lord Jesus Christ. It worked tirelessly to preach the words of the kingdom of heaven, resolutely walked to the cross, forming a complete order for mankind to deal with all things.

Abraham was a small and deeply committed life. He obeyed the absolute command of God, but he did not understand that in such a predicament, chose to commit.

Most expansive life of a finite man.

When Abraham entrusted it, he saw that there was indeed provision on the mountain of the Lord, and in the most perplexing place and the most painful time of mankind, stood the great Lamb of God.

Humanity must practice surrender because Christ is the Christ with us, who is both above and parallel to us. The presence of Christ is a more ultimate Trinity order that makes our commitment to our tragic and hopeless state of life a stable solution.

Therefore, there is an important Trinity order proposition here.

- Despise - Review - Entrust

Who does not despise things leads to greed?

Who do not value everything will lead to laziness?

Who does not entrust everything to rational conceit?

A person believes in the presence of Christ slowly practice the balanced Trinity model of thinking and behavior when dealing with the proposition of all things.

Expand Realm

After being drawn by God, realm will become wide enough to accommodate such a Trinity order at the same time.

Those who have the Lord in their hearts not grasp one point and ignore the rest.

As a heavy body, I am lazy, leave my responsibilities behind, escape from the world.

We familiar these ways of life.

Attached to the mountains and rivers, such as the
Buddhist sense of staying away from the world
and escaping into the empty door. A huge tear in
my inner desires.

Who am I ?

A concrete person desires to have more find
nothing satisfy. I cannot use my understanding
to balance the omnipresent tear, I will inevitably
from hypocrisy to some unwarranted aloofness.

I'll fill my world by taking away the land of
others.

As a spiritual order, I will be confused by the
superficial diversity order of place, you will think

that as long as there is enough accommodation, openness.

When you think act overestimated capability, that everything is belongs to your hands, then you will be deeply attracted by the richness of the world, thence that you are finally reluctant to leave this world and forget the absolute existence of God, thus forming your fatal conceit.

All Things Work Together / All Things Are Like Dung

As a person with mental order, as a person with strong mental tension, you will start to overestimate your ability to think and act, you will cross the boundaries of human reason to give an order, and you will gradually forget those propositions that you cannot solve, such as your

birth, your death, such as your inability to deal

with the order of others' minds.

Reach The Truth

Fall into deep despair, two lines of tears alone in

the dark night.

Commit To God

What is the God reward ?

When I learn to commit?

What will I give to God surrender for?

Breaking down the stable Trinity order, find a

series of pervasive one dimensional errors that may exist in the two-way approach of human nature and epistemology.

We can make the necessary analysis of various schools of thought that have appeared in the history of thought, and more accurately point out the advantages and disadvantages, rationality, and loopholes of a thought.

The Buddhism is that it overemphasizes people's contempt for everything in the world people lose their responsibility, passion, and mission. The Buddhism tries to reach eternity by despising, Such an approach miss the fundamental principle that finite people beings must commit to God in the great questions of life.

The standing Buddha is a lazy ignorant expression. Even person really go of everything, It will not be able to reach eternity, because persons beings finite less than one.

In free market economic theory is that it overemphasizes the ability of people to value everything in this world so that people forget the ability to despise and the ability to commit.

If there is no ability to despise, people will be alienated by wealth, and people will become slaves of wealth. Here is no entrustment, the free market theory will gradually evolve into a theory of the kingdom of heaven on the basis of the free market.

Peoples beings forget the absolute command of God, the beautiful theories of the globalized free market will soon become a game of evildoers sitting on the ground the spoils, the world will become a big supermarket, everyone will worship the golden calf, life will become money, people will not then there are living people with souls.

All kinds of discrimination, no matter how big how small, we keep analyzing.

One Dimensional

That is fatal mistake.

Living alone in this lively planet, with every word is gone, not easy for us to handle our lives well.

I have to meditate the self truth.

Toil/Sorrow/Storms

What Is Reason Falling Into Mediocre Stupidity?

Strive to Write Beautiful Profound Sentence

The thing of value in man is the soul only.

Augustine even said that the only force holding the order of the universe is the soul and not the thing.

The stars have no soul, the mountains and rivers have no soul, the soul is in the conscience of human beings, and God gave human conscience by blowing the breath of life.

This is the most special gift, the miracle that is inherent in each of us. Therefore, a person's thinking and writing must return to the interior *of human nature, to the hometown of the soul,*

otherwise thinking and writing are meaningless.

Unless we know that we are arrogant, ambitious,

greedy, incompetent, miserable, and unrighteous,

we are truly blind. If someone knows all this but

doesn't want to be saved by God, what else is

there to discuss. — Pascal

After listening to the gospel of God, the important

work is to thoroughly doubt yourself. Don't

overestimate your confidence, don't

underestimate your shamelessness. He who

admits that his faith is not enough is the blessed

one who has open-ended error correction.

Bragging about your confidence will inevitably

cover up the filth in your heart. Lies have become

their core technology, and hypocrisy has become

their methodology so that we corrupt people

begin to tell lies confidently in the area of faith.

It's already in hell when it's full of lies before God.

Compared to those who can see the cause, those who only see the effect usually have only eyes and no brain.

Pascal's linear order raises questions, is his experience.

Repeatedly ask yourself, do I have a brain?

Expand your questions along the dimension of the cause, and you can systematically and carefully ask seven questions in a row until you either believe or remain silent.

Too many people are on a result-oriented level, they have eyes but no brains, can't see the truth, can only see bread. No soul can be seen, only thighs can be seen. Constructed stupidity inability.

Seven is a number that accommodates the cause. Three is a number that accommodates the solution.

The American institutional design is the separation of powers, which is the solution of the Trinity Model.

Pascal Sense

There are only two kinds of people in this world. One is an upright person who considers himself a sinner; the other is a sinner who considers himself an upright person.

Which one is it?

Position Conscious With Persons

Where Am I?

In modern world, the Democrats in the United States means liberalism. The Republicans means conservatism.

Discuss

American conservatism must go back to the biblical tradition on which is the country was built. Republicans at least retain based on biblical ideas with possess the energy of open error correction. ONLY

A few countries that have formed alliances with the United States also have such error-correcting capabilities in part.

Because of the spillover effect of American values. Most of the countries in Europe are in massive corruption.

China

As for people in Asia Region. The concept of freedom, equality, and fraternity has not been established, and it belongs to the state of animal tribes.

Marxism and popular liberalism, including the liberalism of the Democratic Party in the United States, the liberalism of most European countries, the political liberalism of equality for it, and the market liberalism that presupposes human selfishness as a virtue, are the Thinking and action unfolding in the first idea system.

Because these thoughts and actions are in a one-dimensional state of ideas, they collectively forget the guilt and rogue attributes of human beings and the inherent powerlessness of human nature.

When they one-dimensionally promote the freedom that people understand Equality and fraternity, they rightly fell into a utopian catastrophe that led humanity down the road of servitude.

Conservative ideological resources in a decentralized order often have the first two concept systems, that is, believe in freedom, equality, and fraternity, and believe that everyone is a scoundrel, but on the proposition entrusted to God, they are self-pity and depend on each other.

Abandon

The situation of this concept leads to conservatism also making huge mistakes in varying degrees.

There is an unspeakable rational conceit in every human being because human existence must emphasize a definite meaning. However, because conservatism has a traditional habit of bowing its head and praying, it does not overestimate people's rational ability, so conservatism will have a periodic error correction ability, so as not to make things out of control. This is the most *fascinating aspect of conservative thinking and, in a sense, the reason for their invincibility.*

Christians

They are very humble and consider themselves completely ignorant, which constitutes a striking sense of ignorance. Admit that you are in a "finite-state" before God.

This is for God's word revelation, not enlightenment and education.

The biblical tradition's conceptual order of human value is a comprehensive order consisting of three conceptual systems:

The first is liberty, equality, and fraternity (a).

The second is that everyone is guilty and everyone is a scoundrel (b).

The third is that each man is powerless to save himself, and man cannot save himself, so it must be handed over to God ©.

The three systems must exist at the same time to form a stable Trinity value model: a+b+c=1.

We are three/ We are one.